100 Plus Educational Strategies to Teach Children of Color

by Jawanza Kunjufu

African American Images

First Edition, First Printing

Front cover illustration by Harold Carr, Jr.

Copyright © 2008 by Jawanza Kunjufu

Printed in the United States of America

10-Digit ISBN #: 1-934155-11-X
13-Digit ISBN #: 978-1-934155-11-0

CONTENTS

DEDICATION

To all teachers who sincerely care about children and want to make a difference in their lives.

To my two late mentors, Dr. Barbara Sizemore and Dr. Asa Hilliard. They truly understood what it meant to be an educator.

CHAPTER 1: FRAMEWORK

Over my almost 35 year career providing school in-service workshops, I have been asked countless times to provide solutions to the problems teachers are encountering in their classrooms. It's as if teachers do not want to understand theory, philosophy, values, or culture. They just want a quick fix pill. In essence they're saying, "Dr. Kunjufu, in this one-hour workshop, if you can just give me ten solutions, I'll be satisfied. I don't need to understand the history, culture, values, and challenges affecting my children. I just want a ten-step process."

In fact, I offer many solutions but only after providing some context about children of color. I insist on providing context because I believe that to teach children you must know them. If you don't know them, chances are you won't like them. I can offer all the solutions in the world, but if you don't like or respect children, if you don't want to teach in a African American or Hispanic school, or if your first choice was to teach in an affluent school in a White suburb, you won't be effective in a classroom with African American/Hispanic students.

You'll find that the strategies and activities I offer will not be effective if you have a negative attitude toward children of color.

In several of my earlier books on education, I mention that in low achieving schools the most negative room in the school is not where the students are. It's the teachers' lounge. Ironically, the same teachers that make derogatory comments about our children in the teachers' lounge are the first to ask me for quick fix solutions to their students' problems.

Primarily I wrote this book for White female teachers. Eighty-three percent of elementary school teachers in America are White and female. The future of children of color lies in the hands of White female teachers.

Since the 1954 Brown vs. Topeka school integration decision, there has been a 66 percent decline in African American teachers. Only six percent of America's teachers are African American, and only one percent are African American males. Thus, I spend around three days a week nationwide primarily working with White female teachers.

I have grown to understand and have compassion for their plight. It's not fair to blame a White female teacher who grew up in a predominately White neighborhood, who attended a college where the education department offered few if any classes on Black/Hispanic history, culture, or learning styles. The same teacher then student taught in a predominately White school, but unfortunately (for her) she was not given her first choice to teach in a predominately White school district. Now she's working in an inner city school with a principal who did not properly provide her with culturally sensitive in-service training. Nor was she assigned a mentor.

This White female college graduate is now teaching in an inner city school, and she's not prepared. It's not her fault. Over my career, I have spent an awful lot of time working with White female teachers. I really appreciate that many sincerely want to make a difference in the lives of African American and Hispanic children.

Several years ago I wrote a book entitled *Black Students, Middle Class Teachers.* Note the title was not *Black Students, White Teachers.* It's sad, but many African American teachers are not connected with African American students. It's amazing how some will send their children to private schools but are against choice for low income children. There's a lot of self-hatred and hypocrisy.

The issue is race and class.

Many middle-class African American teachers have forgotten from whence they came. They need to be reminded that they are DuBois' Talented Tenth. DuBois challenged the Talented Tenth to give back to the least of these.

Types of Teachers

Over my career, I've observed six types of teachers:
1. Custodians
2. Referral Agents
3. Missionaries
4. Instructors
5. Teachers
6. Coaches

Custodians. Custodians often tell students, "I have mine and you have yours to get." They tell colleagues, "I have one year, four months, three weeks, two days, and I'm out of here." These teachers graduated 30 years ago and are using the same lesson plans 30 years later.

Custodians are the most vocal seekers of quick fix solutions in my workshops. They sincerely believe they can implement my solutions while keeping their same old negative attitude and beliefs about children.

Referral Agents. Referral Agents are always seeking ways to reduce the student-teacher ratio. They've found that the most effective method is referring students to special education and suspension.

Twenty percent of teachers make 80 percent of the referrals to special education. Why is it that a child who was not labeled ADD or ADHD by a previous teacher is, all of a sudden, labeled as such by the current Referral Agent? Is the problem with the student or the Referral Agent?

Missionaries. Usually trained in elite schools, Missionaries mean well, but deep down they believe African American/Hispanic students are culturally deprived, broken, and need to be fixed. Of course they have the solution: teach them European culture and values. This is reminiscent of how Africans and Native Americans were force fed European culture. If they were caught enjoying their own culture, they were beaten or killed. What these well-meaning classroom Missionaries do not understand is that they impose a kind of death sentence upon our children when they refuse to teach them anything about African American/ Hispanic culture or history.

Ironically, some Missionaries have visited Africa and made the decision to teach in an inner city school because of their experiences there.

The most zealous Missionaries seldom ask for my assistance. They're not interested in my strategies because they believe their Eurocentric curriculum will save African American/Hispanic children.

The synonym for culture is lifestyle. Everyone has a culture, but arrogant people assume that if you don't have *their* culture, you are deprived.

Missionaries don't last long in the public school system. Most will teach one to five years.

Instructors. Instructors believe they teach subjects, not children. They sincerely believe they teach algebra and English. They don't realize that for Black and Latino students, there can be no significant learning until they first establish a significant relationship.

In several of my books I discuss the Fourth Grade Syndrome. From the fourth grade on, African American/Hispanic scores begin to decline. There are many reasons for this, including the fact that students are increasingly subjected to uncaring Instructors and departmentalization as they get older.

From the fourth grade on, students might have four to seven classes taught by four to seven different Instructors. Instructors do not value the role of self-esteem, motivation, and values in the learning process. They are solely concerned about delivering their subject matter.

I've found that Instructors seem to be concentrated at the high school level. Instructors do not seem interested in my strategies because their one goal is to deliver content. That there are students on the receiving end of their lectures doesn't seem to concern them at all. Thus, they are easily frustrated when, for example, they attempt to teach ninth grade algebra to students who have not mastered their multiplication tables or Shakespeare to students who are not reading at grade level.

Master Teachers understand subject matter as well as the variety of student learning styles. You cannot teach the way you want to teach; you must teach the way children learn.

In the first week of school, Master Teachers ascertain which students are left and right brain learners. This information will dictate what percentage of their lesson plan will be left and right brain. Unfortunately, many Instructors, Custodians, Referral Agents, and Missionaries use left brain lesson plans with right brain thinking students.

We could improve Black and Latino math scores if we provided more right brain lesson plans. I encourage you to read *How to Teach Math to Black Students* for more details.

I love working with Master Teachers in my workshops. They appreciate the role of history, culture, values, and social issues in learning. They have mastered the art of adapting their pedagogy to a variety of student learning styles. They are equally interested in strategies and solutions. My workshops with Teachers and Coaches are my favorites because we learn from each other.

Coaches. Like Instructors, Coaches understand subject matter. Like Teachers, they have mastered congruence between pedagogy and learning styles.

Most importantly, they understand that you cannot teach a child you do not respect, love, or understand.

Coaches understand that there can be no significant learning until a significant relationship is established first. The ability to bond with students is one of their greatest skills. I have been blessed to meet many fantastic Coaches.

The African American Family

It is important for White female teachers to understand that the Black family is not monolithic. In *The Cosby Show*, Bill Cosby played a doctor and his wife, a lawyer. Many people in White America had a difficult time accepting a Black family like the Huxtables.

The reality is that more than 25 percent of African American families earn more than $75,000 per year. Unfortunately, 24 percent of African American families live below the poverty line. And then there are the 51 percent in the middle.

Which Black family are you talking about: *The Cosby Show* families earning more than $75,000, the *Good Times* families living below the poverty line, or the *Roc* families of the middle class?

Many races view the Black family as monolithic. That's why we often hear the statement, "You're different!" This statement is made when a White person meets an African

American who graduated from Harvard or who wants to be on the debate team or who does not fit any of the stereotypes of African Americans. When they say, "You're not like them!" what they really mean is that they're so racist they can only see African American people from one vantage point. When an African American does not reinforce their stereotypes, they're different from "all" other members of their race.

Of the 40 million Americans who live below the poverty line, 24 million are White. You'd never know this watching television. For some reason the networks can find the 16 million poor Blacks and Latinos who are concentrated in urban jungles, but they can't find the 24 million poor Whites who are scattered throughout rural America.

How can racists digest the fact that 76 percent of all drug users are White? Ironically, 70 percent of those convicted for possession are Black and Latino. Is there a war on drugs, or is there a war on Blacks and Latinos?

The Framework

Changing your beliefs, stereotypes, and attitudes about African American/Hispanic students can be a difficult process. The strategies and activities in this book may challenge your beliefs at the most fundamental level. Yet for the sake of our children, I encourage you to keep an open mind and consider implementing as many of the strategies and activities as you can.

The following four stages of this process of attitudinal change form a theoretical framework you can use to assess your own thoughts and feelings as you read the material and plan your course of action:

- Denial
- Admit
- Understand
- Appreciate.

Denial. I'll never forget when a White female teacher in Seattle told me, "I don't see

13

color. I see children as children." Teachers can tell me anything in a sterile auditorium, but bulletin boards, library collections, and classroom décor tell me all I need to know about what teachers really think of their students.

After my workshop, I asked this teacher if I could visit her classroom. The racial breakdown of students was 60 percent African American, 20 percent Hispanic, 10 percent Asian, and 10 percent White. When I walked into her classroom I saw an all-White Dick and Jane library collection, pictures of famous White Americans hanging on the walls, and posters of White children. Yet she didn't see color. I believe she saw color better than anyone else!

Denial is probably my biggest adversary when trying to work with teachers, Black or White, male or female.

Admit. Teachers must finally admit that culture and race are factors in their students' academic performance. This may be difficult for some educators to admit. It's a humbling experience to admit when you're wrong or that you don't know everything about African American children. The classic statement is, "I don't see color. I see children as children." Many teachers think they're liberal when they make this statement. I believe the statement shows their naiveté and covers their racism.

Understand. Teachers must at least try to understand their students' culture. White female teachers are assigned African American/ Hispanic classrooms in the inner city, but they are not given one course in Black/Hispanic history, culture, or learning styles. Thus, it is your responsibility to learn on your own. My workshops and books, along with those of my peers, address this issue to help teachers understand the culture.

You must also stay abreast of developments in education. We work in a dynamic field, yet many educators do not subscribe to trade journals, magazines, and newspapers. What books have you read in the past six months on your subject or education in general? How can teachers call themselves educators and not read the literature in their field? Everyday a new scientific discovery is made, a new math formula is devised. Even in the field of history new discoveries are constantly challenging the Eurocentric view of the world. I strongly encourage all teachers to read *Education Week, Journal of Negro Education,* and *Education Leadership.* Also, you should read all of the books related to the psychology and education of African American/Hispanic children.

Appreciate. The third stage is to appreciate the culture. You can be African American and not appreciate the culture. I believe that people like Clarence Thomas and Ward Connerlly, who are African American, don't really appreciate African American culture.

Throughout this book, we will offer strategies and activities to help African American/Hispanic children appreciate their culture. For example, Black History Month should not be confined to the month of February. Hispanic month should not be confined to September 15th - October 15th. It should be taught 365 days per year. Appreciating the culture is more than asking Black children to wear native attire, bring in native music and food, and throw a party. Black culture is far more than dress, music, and food.

Immerse yourself in the literature of your students. Subscribe to *Ebony* and *Hispanic* magazines. Read *The Destruction of Black Civilization*, *Before the Mayflower*, *America's Latinos* and *Handbook of Hispanic Cultures*.

Watch two very contrasting television shows: *106 & Park* and *Tony Brown's Journal*. This will clearly reinforce the reality that the African American community is not monolithic.

Visit a Black/Hispanic church. It is our largest institution and has the greatest influence on the African American community.

Also visit a Black college, especially Morehouse, Spelman, Xavier, Howard, Tuskegee, Hampton, and North Carolina A&T.

Pop Quiz

I'd like you to take the following multicultural quiz. Before I offer you my 100 Plus strategies and activities, let's ascertain how well versed you are in the history and culture of your students.

Multicultural Quiz

1. How do African American children define good hair and pretty eyes?
2. Why do many African American youth associate beauty with light skin?
3. What are the benefits of dark skin?
4. Name some classical Black/Hispanic musicians and writers.
5. Why do some African American/Hispanic youth associate being smart with acting White?

6. Why don't Whites associate being smart with acting Black or Hispanic?
7. At what age do Jewish parents and educators teach their children about the Holocaust?
8. At what age do parents and educators of African American children teach them about slavery?
9. From a multicultural perspective, what is the difference between a salad bowl and a melting pot?
10. Why did twentieth-century European immigrants melt into American society faster than African Americans?
11. What makes countries Third World? What are the first and second worlds?
12. Who built the Pyramids? When were they built? When was the zenith of Greek civilization?
13. What is Standard English?
14. Did Oakland schools want to teach African American students Ebonics?
15. What is code switching?

16. What percentage of the world population is White?
17. What is the one-drop-of-blood theory?
18. How many Whites live below the poverty line in America?
19. What percentage of drug users and drug convictions involve Whites?
20. Which day of the week and hour are the most segregated in America?
21. Do you have different opinions when you see four African American/Hispanic male teens in the school hallway versus four White male teens?
22. What is the difference between a group and a gang? Between being assertive and aggressive?

Unfortunately, teachers are prepared to work with *Leave It To Beaver* children, not BeBe's kids. Most college education departments prepare teachers to work with self-motivated children whose parents have made education the primary issue in the family.

But what if students lack the motivation to learn? Students must be convinced that education is important, and you must compete with media, from music videos to video games. Children are viewed as consumers, and everyone is trying to sell them something.

Everyday teachers stand before children who lack motivation. You must see yourself, not just as an educator but as a sales person, a marketer who is promoting and advertising a product called *education*.

Custodians, Referral Agents, Missionaries, and Instructors are unsuccessful in the classroom because they haven't accepted that they must become a promoter of education. They'll tell you that sales is not part of their job description. They never learned this aspect of the job in college, so therefore it is unnecessary. However, if you want to be effective in this 21st century, with Black and Latino students in particular, it behooves you to understand that you must sell your product.

After all is said and done, whatever you see in the child is what you'll produce out of the child. You have to like children to teach them. You have to like African American children. You have to like Hispanic children. You have to like a Black male dressed in hip hop gear with an angry scowl on his face. You have to like dark skinned children with short hair who did not wash up or brush their teeth. You have to convince children that who they are is more important than their performance. You have to convince your children that they are important to you. They are special. You value them, you sincerely care about them.

I can quickly evaluate a teacher by observing how the children respond to them. Children know if you like them or not. They do not possess a PhD, but they know when teachers care about them and when they don't. Interestingly, teachers who do not care about our children demand the most quick fix solutions.

You have to treat children with dignity and respect. You can't treat children with dignity and respect if you don't care about them.

So many teachers are burning out, and it's not just because of lack of support from principals and parents or lack of income. If you can only ask students what you already know students will only know what you know. You've done the basics of your job. However, wouldn't it be exciting if, from time to time, students felt comfortable and confident enough to teach *you* something? This can only happen if you have bonded with students, they trust you, you feel secure within yourself, and if you ask open-ended questions. If you want to train children, ask questions with predetermined answers. If you want to educate a child, ask open-ended questions that stimulate creative and critical thought.

When you ask open-ended questions, you become a facilitator of knowledge. You have to feel comfortable with the idea that you may not know the answer to the questions you've asked. One of the best ways to avoid burn out is to be a facilitator, where you are always a student and everyone in the classroom learns from each other.

Teachers who use the same lesson plans year after year are at high risk of burn out. Refresh your lesson plans. Set a goal that every year, at least 20 percent of your lesson plans will feature new material.

You can avoid burn out if you continue to grow.

Now we'll move into the purpose of this book: to present strategies and activities that are designed to solve many of the problems students and teachers are facing in today's inner city classroom. No more theory. No more philosophy. Just concrete strategies that you can implement to make your classroom an exciting learning experience for youth.

CHAPTER 2: BONDING

1.

Put your desk in the center of the classroom. To be a facilitator of knowledge, you need to be in the center of the class. This will also reduce the distance between you and students who sit in the back of the room. By being in the center of the room, you are in closer proximity to all of your students. Unfortunately, this solution may be a little more challenging in those schools where the desks are bolted to the floor.

2.

Hang a picture of yourself on the wall—only this picture is from your childhood, when you were in the same grade you're currently teaching. Students need to realize that you were not always an adult, that you were once a child.

3.

Get to know your students—their goals, dreams, and desires. Have them write down what they'd like to be when they're 30 years old. Remind them of their goal throughout the school year.

4.

Make sure assignments are not too easy, or students will get bored. Also, make sure assignments are not too hard, or they'll give up.

5.

Call your students by their surnames: Mr.

_____ and Miss _____. A classroom

atmosphere of dignity and respect is created

by how you treat your students. I just love

seeing a primary grade teacher address her

students as Mr. _____ and Miss _____.

6.

Hug, smile, encourage, and shake the hands of students. As students walk into the classroom, greet them at the door and give them a hug, smile, word of encouragement, or handshake.

7.

Proximity. Research shows that some teachers avoid getting close to students they don't like. Throughout the day, make sure you are in close proximity to all of your students and that each student receives some form of touch or a word of encouragement from you.

8.

The power of words: praise and criticism. Understand the power of words. Promise yourself that you will never say anything negative about your students. Keep a daily chart of the number of times you praise the child vs. criticize. Children want attention, and unfortunately, many have found they receive more attention being negative than being positive.

9.

Apologize. Children respect teachers more when they apologize. Share with your students some of the mistakes you made when you were their age. Children need to see you as human, as a person, just like them.

10.

Dress like a professional. If you want your children to respect you, you need to dress like a professional. Sometimes when I go into schools, it's hard for me to distinguish the teachers from the students because both are dressed in blue jeans and t-shirts. I'm concerned about educators in America who say, "I'm just a teacher." In Germany, Japan, and Ghana, there's no one more respected than a teacher. They understand that whatever you want to be—engineer, lawyer, doctor—you'll gain that knowledge from a teacher. In those and many other countries, educators dress like professionals.

11.

Call parents with good news. Many parents say the only time they hear from the school is when something negative has taken place with their child. Just as we want you to give good news to students, we also want you to give good news to parents. Once a month or once a quarter, I encourage you to call your parents with some good news.

12.

Visit each home. I was taught that you should never assign homework until you have a very good idea of where your work is going to be done. This is also an excellent time for you to bond with parents and students, because they know this is not part of your job description. You've gone beyond the call of duty in making a home visit. Some school districts are now requiring home visits because this is something most teachers do not want to do.

13.

Hold monthly parent meetings in your room and serve a potluck dinner. Can you imagine, you may be able to attract more parents to your room than the school PTA? Once a month, have a meeting with parents. Food is an excellent way to attract parents. Make it a potluck dinner so that you're not assuming the total financial burden. Students will be involved in academic activities—playing chess, checkers, dominos, computer activities—while you meet with parents. This is an excellent opportunity to ask each parent to volunteer one day per month to help you in the classroom.

14.

Business dress day. We must teach our children to be professional. Once a month, have your children dress in formal attire. Teach them to act like gentlemen and ladies. Invite a role model to come and speak to the students. Take a field trip to a nice sit-down restaurant. Some of our children have only been to fast food places. They've never experienced a five-course meal with a waiter serving them. If there are any students who have difficulty securing a dress shirt and tie or a nice dress, ask your parents or the larger community for assistance.

15.

Stay after school. If you can stay for an extra 30 minutes to an hour after school, you can offer extracurricular activities, such as clubs (dance, martial arts, debate team, science fair, computer). Students can do their homework. They can volunteer to develop a newsletter or run a classroom store. Bonding occurs when students see you involved in their lives beyond the call of duty and your job description. You can also use this time for yourself. You can grade papers, develop new lesson plans, and decorate your bulletin board.

16.

Weekend activities. Each weekend, take one or two of your students on an outing. For example, you can go to church, a museum, Great America, a ballgame, or the zoo. When students know this is going to be their weekend to be with their teacher, this creates a wonderful moment they'll remember forever.

CHAPTER 3: DÉCOR

17.

Ask students to bring in a current photo and hang around the room, because your students are the stars of your class. If you've done your bonding exercises, then you'll know what your students want to be when they grow up. Find posters of famous African Americans/Hispanics that work in the same careers and put them next to the appropriate children. For example, if David wants to be a doctor, then find a picture of someone like Dr. Ben Carson and put his photo next to David's.

18.

Have positive music playing in the background. Play different genres of music. Children need to know there's more to music than just hip hop. So hip hop can play on Monday while jazz, classical, gospel, R&B, latin, reggae and mariachi can play on the other days (quietly in the background). Not only will this make the learning experience more enjoyable, but research has shown that certain genres of music can stimulate cognitive development and reduce behavioral problems.

19.

If at all possible, have all of your chairs in a circle. There is excellent research on the value of a circle. Facilitators operate best in a circle.

20.

Put *all* student names on the board. In many classrooms, the board carries a negative connotation. Teachers put students' names on the board if they've been acting out. In this system, students work their way onto the board (thus gaining negative attention). Let's turn this around. Let all children be featured on the board under a big sign that says "Stars" (thus gaining positive attention). If a student acts out, his name is taken off the board (symbolically exiling him). I once visited a classroom, and as early as 9:15, three students were on the board (old system) for acting up. I asked the teacher, "How long will the names be on the board?" She said, "All day." So you know how they acted the rest of the day. The behaviors we want more of are the ones we should reinforce the most. Rather than a negative board, let's create a positive board. Moreover, if students change their behavior, their names are placed back on the board (redemption).

21.

Provide a classroom that's full of life. Why are some upper grade classrooms so drab and dry? Living, breathing children die in these classrooms. Liven up your classroom with plants, a fishbowl, flowers (live or artificial)— whatever can be done to provide a lively classroom experience.

22.

Gifted and talented area. If you don't have a gifted and talented area in your classroom, create one today and hang a big sign that says, "Gifted and Talented." Fill it up with academic games, puzzles, books, magazines, computers, and other academic activities so that when fast learners finish their assignments before the rest of the class, rather than acting up, they can go to this great area of the room to immerse themselves in all the fun activities you have provided.

23.

Geography: Display the Peters Map. We need to quit lying to children. America is not the same size as Africa. America is not in the center of the world. Europe is not a continent; it does not have water on all sides. There are only six continents, not seven. The most accurate map is the Peters Map. Call African American Images at 800-552-1991 to purchase our SETCLAE curriculum, in which the Peters Map is featured.

24.

Talk to parents about reducing TV time and increasing study time. Create a poster with the information below.

Students	SAT Scores	Study Time	Television Time
Asians	1600	12 hrs/wk	2 hrs/wk
Whites	1582	8 hrs/wk	4 hrs/wk
Hispanics	1371	2 hrs/wk	30 hrs/wk
African Americans	1291	1 hr/wk	38 hrs/wk

Whatever you do most will be what you do best.

25.

Teach your students the real deal about getting an NBA contract. Create a poster with the information below.

– 1 million athletes desire to get into the NBA or WNBA.

– There are 100,000 new high school positions.

– There are 4,000 new college positions.

– There are 35 new NBA/WNBA positions.

– There are 7 new starting positions.

– Average career: 4 years.

26.

African American students fantasize about becoming rich rappers. Show them how quickly their millions can evaporate. Create a poster with the information below.

– 1 million CDs sell for $18 = $18 million.

– Distributors get 50 percent = $9 million.

– Producers get 40 percent = $7.2 million.

– Studio and video costs = $800,000.

– IRS gets 50 percent = $500,000.

– Rapper buys Bentley for $500,000.

– Rapper ends up with $0.

27

Deglamorize the life of the drug dealer. Create a poster with the information below.

– Drug Dealers

– $10,000 best day

– $700 month average

– $8,400 year income

– 3 year average career before:

- They use drugs

- Go to jail

- Die

28.

Create classroom learning centers. There are five ways to learn: writing, oral, pictures, fine arts, and artifacts. Create five different learning centers that feature activities using each method. Dedicate one day out of the week to learning centers. On learning center day, children can move from one center to another. Observe where students linger. This will tell you a lot about their unique learning styles. Unfortunately, many Instructors from the fourth grade on only use the written approach with ditto sheets and text books. Try going every Monday without using a ditto sheet and every Friday without using a text book.

29.

A high school dropout earns $6.00 per hour.
A high school graduate earns $8.00 per hour.
A college graduate earns $20.00 per hour.
A graduate degree earns $40 per hour.

Convince students that education pays. Many Blacks and Hispanics believe the odds are better in the NBA, rap, and drug dealing than with a good education and working hard. You must do everything within your power to convince students that education pays. Invite African and Hispanic role models with degrees to speak to students. Include their pictures, articles, and books in the presentation to make a strong case for the value of education.

30.

Encourage students to ask, "Why do we have to learn this?" Never leave a lesson without first showing the relationship between the theoretical concept and something that's relevant to their experience.

31.

Hey Black Child

Hey Black Child

Do ya know who ya are

Who ya really are

Do ya know you can be

What ya wanna be

If ya try to be

What ya can be

Hey Black Child

Do ya know where ya goin

Where ya really goin

Do ya know you can learn

What ya wanna learn

What ya can learn

Hey Black Child

Do ya know ya are strong

I mean really strong

Do ya know you can do

What ya wanna do

If ya try to do

What ya can do

Hey Black Child

Be what ya can be

Learn what ya must learn

Do what ya can do

And tomorrow your nation

Will be what ya want it to be

(Replace Black with Hispanic depending on your students)

32.

Teach students the following order of success:

- diploma

- degree

- career

- marriage

- children.

Create a poster with the information.

33.

Career development. Ask your students what they want to be when they're 30 years old. Write down the careers next to the students' names in your record book. Refer to your children by their career for the rest of the school year (Pilot Jones, Dr. Smith, Attorney Bailey). Have your students write a different career for each letter of the alphabet. Bring in as much literature as possible on careers.

34.

College application forms. Students need to be motivated to pursue college as early as possible. Early in the school year, hand out a college application form to each of your students, even kindergarteners. They should complete the forms in class and/or at home. All must be returned to you for a grade. In your Gifted and Talented area, place college brochures on the walls and tables. If possible, during the school year, field trips should be taken to local colleges. During spring break or summer vacation, students should visit colleges, preferably Black colleges.

35.

Talk to students about Dr. Ben Carson. Dr. Carson grew up in low income, single parent home, and his mother didn't finish school. Many of your students will relate to Dr. Carson's childhood. They need to know that if Dr. Ben Carson—an African American from a poor, single parent home—could become a success, they can, too.

36.

Positive attributes. Give each student small sheets of paper for the total number of students in the class. If you have 28 students, then each will be given 28 small sheets of paper. They are to write one to three positive attributes about each of their fellow classmates. We must teach our children to see the positive in each other. Upon completion, compile all the attributes so that each child has a list of all attributes written by their classmates.

37.

A lesson in making choices. Ask students, "If you had a Bentley, all the clothes you could ever wear, a 30 bedroom mansion, time, 100,000 acres of land, and $1 million, which would you value the most?" Help them to see that the most important choice out of the six would be time.

38.

Attitude

The longer I live, the more I realize the impact of attitude on life. Attitude, to me, is more important than facts. It is more important than the past, than education, than money, than circumstances, than failures, than success, than what other people think or say or do. It is more important than appearance, gifts, or skills. It will make or break a company...a church...a home. The remarkable thing is we have a choice every day regarding the attitude we will embrace for that day. We cannot change our past...we cannot change the fact that people will act in a certain way. We cannot change the inevitable. The only thing we can do is pray on the one string we have, and that is our attitude. I am convinced that life is 10 percent what happens to me and 90 percent how I react to it.

39.

Self history. Before we talk about the history of the nation and world, let's first have students develop an historical timeline of their lives. For example, let's say your students are around 10 years old. On a sheet of paper, have them put their baby picture and the date of their birth, a picture of when they were around five, and a picture of them now. This timeline is also a part of history. The same applies to geography. Before we show the geography and map of the world, let's show maps of our classroom, neighborhood, and students' homes. They can show the four directions using the classroom, the neighborhood, and their homes.

40.

Psychology of performance. Winning or losing can be attributed to one of four factors: ability, effort, luck, and the nature of the task. When students with strong self-esteem do well on a quiz, they attribute their success to ability or effort made. If students with strong self-esteem do poorly on a test, they never question their ability. They realize they're always in control. All they have to do is study harder. That's how winners think, and we must constantly reinforce this mindset within students. Unfortunately, students with low self-esteem attribute doing well on an exam to luck or the nature of the task (it was easy). They attribute poor performance to low ability. Too many African American/Hispanic students have convinced themselves they're not well versed in math and science. They question their ability. When going over assignments and tests with students, stress that all students have the ability to succeed. The only difference between students with good grades and students with poor grades is the amount of time and effort given to studying the material. Luck has nothing to do with it.

41.

Give your students two grades: one for effort, one for achievement. We must convince students of the importance of effort. Self-esteem and self-confidence can be enhanced with this approach.

42.

Have weekly spelling bees and math contests. Academics should be fun. Encourage students to bring just as much excitement to spelling bees, math contests, Black/Hispanic history bowls, and quizzes as they bring to sports and rap concerts. It would be great if a sponsor like McDonald's or a local pizza restaurant provided prizes to the winning students.

43.

Rule 110: the race card. Many African American/ Hispanic students have been playing the wrong card. They play the race card like this: "Come on, teacher, help a brother out. I'm Black/Hispanic, I'm poor, I'm from a single parent home." They're playing the wrong card. Many students try to make teachers (especially White teachers) feel guilty enough to compromise and lower their standards. Before integration and several years after Brown vs. Topeka, the rule was 110. Teachers used to tell Black students, "Because the country is racist, you need to score more than 80, 90, 100. You have to be the best. You have to score 110." We must teach our children which race card to play. Not the victim card, but the 110 card. Whenever a student plays the victim card, remind him that he's playing the wrong card. Tell him, "The only card played in our classroom is card 110."

44.

Teach students that being smart is *not* acting White. Many African American/Hispanic students associate being smart with acting White. They associate speaking proper English with speaking White. We must turn the table on that logic and convince students that being smart is acting Black/Hispanic. Speaking proper English is acting Black/Hispanic.

45.

Combat miseducation around hair and pretty eyes. Too many African American children, for a myriad of reasons, have been taught that good hair is long and straight and that pretty eyes are anything but dark brown. The lighter you are, the prettier you are. Flood your room with positive pictures of dark skinned males and females with curly hair to reinforce students' beauty and intelligence.

Entrepreneurship

46.

Have students write a business plan. We need to quit telling children to get a good education to get a good job. Let's use the combination of language arts and mathematics to help children develop a business plan. The business plan would answer the following questions:

– What is your product or service?

– How do you plan to market and advertise your business?

– How much capital is required?

– What are the qualifications to develop your product or service?

– What type of staffing is needed?

– What is the expected level of profit?

47.

Teach students about the stock market. Have half the class buy Nike shoes and the other half buy Nike stock. Have the class evaluate both at year end. Give your students $100 in play money at the beginning of the year. They will invest the $100 in a particular stock. Periodically throughout the school year, they'll monitor the growth of the stock. There will be a prize given to the student whose stock appreciated the most by year end.

48.

Teach students about real estate. Take a walking field trip around the neighborhood and explain to students how every piece of property, including land, is owned by someone. There's more to life than just standing on the corner. Teach students to own the corner. Show them the cost of housing in their neighborhood. Have them investigate how much it would cost to purchase property for sale or in foreclosure, how much it would cost to rehab it, then sell it. If you can get a real estate investor or developer to sponsor an after school project, students could learn how to purchase properties, fix them up, and sell them. The proceeds would go to them.

49.

The Booker T. Washington-W.E.B. DuBois Program. Weekly or monthly, invite a positive role model. Alternate between blue collar and white collar role models. We must show children the value in both blue collar and white collar skills.

CHAPTER 5: HISTORY

50.

This day in Black/Hispanic history. History should not be confined to one month. Every day, share a Black/Hispanic history fact with your students. As a resource, purchase a Black/Hispanic history calendar or history book. Everyday, begin your one-minute history break by saying, "This day in Black/Hispanic history...."

51.

Discuss modern Africa. Show your students a video or pictures from *National Geographic* of modern Africa. Too many children think Africa is made up huts and jungles alone. They need to see hotels, skyscrapers, highways, restaurants, cars, schools, hospitals, and the industry of Africa.

52.

Share the wonder of ancient Egypt with students. Africans built many pyramids and your students need to know that. The Giza pyramid is one of the Seven Wonders of the World. People today are still trying to figure out how an ancient people could have built a monument that's 48 stories high, 755 feet wide, and contains 2,300,000 stones. The stones weigh three tons each, and they are perfectly balanced. Some researchers even believe the dimensions and geographical orientation of the Giza Pyramid relate to certain star systems in the cosmos, which means that in addition to mathematics, engineering, construction, and architecture, they had to know astronomy. The pyramids were built around 2780 B.C. Pythagoras was born later in 600 B.C., and Hippocrates was born 500 B.C. How did those Africans do it without the help of Europeans?

53.

Discuss the slave revolts. There were more than 246 slave revolts. Children need to know that their ancestors did not accept slavery. Hang pictures and provide information about Harriet Tubman, Denmark Vesey, Gabriel Prosser, and Henry Highland Garnett. Teach them that over 30 million Africans died during slavery.

54.

Understand the connection between the Willie Lynch letter and student behavior.

Willie Lynch Letter

Gentlemen, I greet you here on the banks of the James River in the Year of Our Lord 1712. First, I shall thank you, the gentlemen of the colony of Virginia, for bringing me here. I am here to help you solve some of your problems with slaves.

Your invitation reached me on my modest plantation in the West Indies while experimenting with the newest and still oldest methods for control of slaves. Ancient Rome would envy us if my program is implemented. As our boat sails south on the James River named for the illustrious King James whose Bible we cherish, I find enough to know that your problem is not unique.

While Rome used cords of wood as crosses for standing human bodies along the old highways in great numbers, you are here using the tree and rope on occasion, I caught the whiff of a dead slave hanging from a tree a couple of miles back. You are not only losing valuable stock by hangings, you are having uprisings. Slaves are running away. Your crops are sometimes left in the field too long for maximum profit. You suffer occasional fires. Your animals are killed.

Gentlemen, you know what your problems are. I do not need to elaborate. I am here to provide a method of controlling your black slaves. I guarantee every one of you that installed correctly it will control the slave for at least 300 years. My method is simple. Any member of your family or any overseer can use it.

I have outlined a number of differences among the slaves and I take these differences and make them bigger. I use fear, mistrust, and envy for control purposes. These methods have worked on my modest plantation in the West Indies and they will work throughout the South.

Take this simple little list of differences and think about them. On the top of my list is age, but it is there only because it starts with the letter A. The second is color or shade. There is intelligence, size, sex, size of plantation, attitude of owners, whether the slave lived in the valley, on the hill, east, west, north, south, has fine or coarse hair or is tall or short.

Now that you have a list of differences, I shall give you an outline of action. But before that I shall assure you that distrust is stronger than trust and envy is stronger than adulation, respect, or admiration. The black slave, after receiving this indoctrination, shall carry on and become self-refueling and self-generating for hundreds of years, maybe thousands. Don't forget, you must pitch the old black versus the young black male and the young black male against the old black male. You must use the dark skinned slaves versus the light skinned slaves and the light skinned slaves versus the dark skinned slaves. You must use the female versus the male and the male versus the female. You must also have your servants and overseers distrust all blacks, but it is necessary that your slaves trust and depend on us. They must love, respect, and trust only us.

Gentlemen, these kits are your keys to control. Use them. Have your wives and children use them. Never miss an opportunity. My plan is guaranteed, and the good thing about this plan is that if used intensely for one year, the slaves themselves will remain perpetually distrustful.

Every child needs to know about the Willie Lynch letter. Students should read it, discuss it, analyze it, and write about it. Every time your children act up or disagree or want to argue or fight with each other, have them read the letter. Let this knowledge be your guide when mediating conflict.

55.

Understand the origins and destructiveness of the N word.

The N Word

- The Latin word for Black.
- During slavery and Jim Crow, it was used by Whites to insult African Americans. It was the most negative word to describe a person.
- If African American parents had taught their children their history and culture, they would have a better understanding.
- Unfortunately they did not, so some Hip Hop youth can be heard saying "Wassup, my N_ _ _ _ _?"
- Hip Hop culture has turned the most negative word into a term of endearment: "My N_ _ _ _ _."

- Somehow they know enough about the history of the word to stop others outside the race from using it. They also know enough about the word to use it against a brother or sister you don't like, which is the same way Whites used it 200 years ago. "I hate you Black N_ _ _ _ _." "N_ _ _ _ _ you ain't s_ _ _."

Ask your students:

1) When people outside your race hear you use the word, are they influenced to use it?

2) Do you think you owe your elders the courtesy and respect not to use it?

3) Do you think you have the right to continue to use the word?

56.

Teach the Inclusion Model.

White	Black
Abraham Lincoln	Frederick Douglass
Thomas Edison	Lewis Latimer
Alexander Bell	Granville T. Woods
Eleanor Roosevelt.	Mary McCleod Bethune
Hippocrates	Imhotep
Pythagoras	Ahmose
John F. Kennedy	Martin Luther King
Hillary Clinton	Barack Obama

Teach the Multicultural Model.

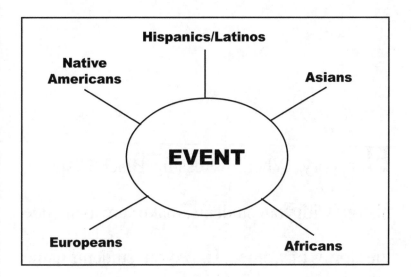

Event

- Columbus comes to America

- Slavery in America

- Concentration camps during World War II

- Immigration

Have each group comment on each event.

58.

Her story. When discussing Black/Hispanic history with your students, make sure to include the stories of women. Have your students name 20 famous women? Note the word *history*. We seem to know more about the contributions of males than females. Challenge your students to learn about women.

59.

Teach your students the Nguzo Saba. Each day review a principle. Students have to reinforce the principle. We can reduce metal detectors and security guards with African values.

Nguzo Saba

1. Unity
2. Self-determination
3. Collective work and responsibility
4. Cooperative economics
5. Purpose
6. Creativity
7. Faith

60.

Teach your students Ma'at. Each day review a principle. Students have to reinforce the principle. We can reduce metal detectors and security guards with African values.

Ma'at

1. Truth

2. Justice

3. Order

4. Harmony

5. Balance

6. Reciprocity

7. Righteousness

CHAPTER 6: LANGUAGE ARTS

61.

Journaling. Every day have your students write at least one page in their journals. This can be done at the beginning of the school day where they write about their experiences from the previous night. Or at the end of the day they can write about what they learned in class. Students should always be asking themselves, "What did I learn today?"

62.

Write letters to government officials. Students should write letters to government officials about problems in their neighborhoods. This is an excellent opportunity to connect writing skills to the reality of their neighborhoods. If your students live in a neighborhood filled with crack houses, they should write anonymous letters to the police department letting them know where the crack houses are located. Have your students write anonymous letters to the police department about crimes that have taken place. The letters should be written anonymously

so they won't feel they're involved in snitching.
Have students write letters to city council
members asking why there are so many liquor
stores and businesses selling drug paraphernalia
in Black/Hispanic communities. Write letters
to the Justice Department asking why there's
such a disparity between the punishments for
crack cocaine and cocaine use.

63.

Have an open mic time. The last five or ten minutes of the school day can be reserved for open mic. Call this 106 & Park after the popular tv show on BET. Children can read their poetry or share hip hop lyrics as long as readings reinforce language arts.

64.

School talk, street talk; Standard English, Black English. Allow a certain time in the day for students to talk in the vernacular of the street (or Black English), but most of the day (90 percent or more) remind them to speak Standard English by saying, "School talk!" Students will learn how to vacillate between the two. Unfortunately, many of our students speak 90 percent street talk/Black English, but they need to be bilingual and learn Standard English to function in society.

65.

The Dozens, Signifying, Cracking, and Ranking. The Dozens is a Black cultural verbal game designed to avoid fighting. The game works because in Black culture, words are a figure of speech. In White culture, words are taken literally. It takes skills to play the Dozens. To play this game well, you must be able to make words rhyme and draw on a vast vocabulary. The best players are witty, comfortable speaking in public, and think quickly on their feet. While you wouldn't allow students to play the Dozens in class, you can draw on the skills. Empower your best Dozens player to be the MC at all your programs. Put him or her on your spelling and debate teams.

66.

Create a newspaper. One of the best ways to reinforce language arts is to empower your students to be reporters. Once a month, have them write an article about something that happened in the school or neighborhood. Encourage them to sell the newspaper to the student body or residents of the community. Encourage them to write articles about positive issues because the media glorifies the negative.

67.

Accommodate right brain learners. If possible, teach math with right brain techniques: oral, pictures, artifacts, or fine arts. Provide as many hands on activities as possible. Connect the integer line to east and west, north and south in the city. Use an abacus. Connect math as much as possible to real live experiences. Use pies, pizzas, and cookies to demonstrate fractions and geometry.

68.

Teach students how to set up and solve word problems. Children often see no connection between math and their lives. They may know how to perform an operation but not how, when, or why to use it in a word problem. Explain why they must learn how to add, subtract, multiply, and divide. Design word problems using NBA math, NFL math, or rap math. If you want to produce an employee, solve the problem for him. If you want to produce an employer, give them word problems that they must set up and solve.

69.

Assign health-oriented science projects. Bring in a piece of pork and put it in a glass of 7 Up so that children can see the worms coming out. Teach students about the body's elimination system. It's not enough to just discuss the parts of the body. We must teach students, from a scientific point of view, how eating habits and lifestyle affect health. Connect science to healthy eating by discussing how long certain foods remain in the colon before being eliminated and why this is a health issue. For example:

– Pork stays 12 to 14 days

– Beef, 8 to 12 days

– Chicken, 6 to 8 days

– Fish, 3 to 5 days

– Fruits and vegetables, 6 hours

70.

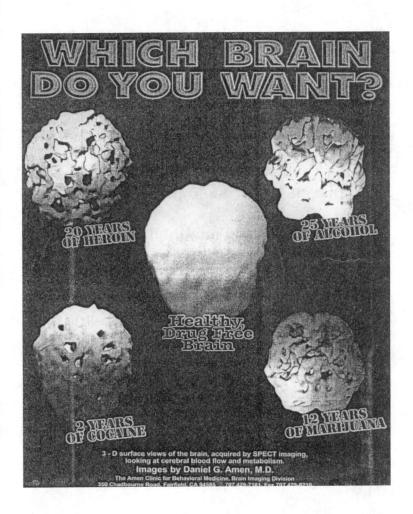

71.

How do things work? The Internet, computers, electricity, iPods, CD players, and DVD players are technological wonders we use everyday. Let's show children how the things they take for granted really work. Have students take apart an old computer and study its component parts. You may be surprised to find that some of your "slow" learners will surpass even your A students in this hands-on activity.

72.

Teach about Black inventors. Using the books *Great Negroes Past and Present, Black Inventors,* and *Blacks in Science and Engineering,* have students list 20 or more things that were invented by African Americans. Have an Invention Fair, where students invent their own technological wonders. The goal of each invention would be to enhance the quality of real life.

CHAPTER 8: DISCIPLINE

73.

Insist that words of respect be used in your classroom. Yes sir, no sir. Yes ma'am, no ma'am. Good morning. Excuse me. I'm sorry. Thank you. You're welcome. We must teach children the importance of these words. Read my book–*A Culture of Respect*.

74.

Don't suspend or refer your most challenging student to special education. There's a good chance your most challenging student is male, angry, and causing disciplinary problems. The best way to correct his behavior is to give him a hug, a smile, and a word of encouragement— on a daily basis.

75.

Have your most challenging student serve as captain of the team. You need to have this student on your side. There's a good chance your best student and your worst student are both male. Males want attention, and you need to find ways to stroke their egos. As captain of the team, this student's responsibility is to pass out papers, clean the blackboard, put up supplies, and take notes to the office. He'll assist you in getting students back on task by being the example.

76.

Don't suspend or refer the class clown to special education. These students are usually male and not doing well in school. He feels like a failure, and as you can imagine, this is difficult to handle. One of the ways underperforming students protect themselves is by becoming the class clown. Understand what the class clown is trying to achieve. He wants to annoy you so much that you'll put him out of class. When the class clown starts acting up, pull him over and say, "There's nothing you can do that would motivate me to put you out of my class. Secondly, since you think you're funny, I'm going to give you a forum, an opportunity to show off your skills the last five or ten minutes of the school day."

You never know. Your student could become the next Chris Rock or Eddie Murphy. He might remember you and give you a portion of his earnings! All because you empowered him to develop and use his skills.

77.

Don't suspend or refer the thug to special education. There's probably a student in your class who wants to intimidate you. He's similar to the class clown in that he wants to be put out of class primarily because he's unable to keep up with the work. We must create an environment in our classrooms where children feel safe to make mistakes. They need to understand that's how you learn. Your safe haven should help thugs and class clowns feel comfortable with being slightly behind their fellow students.

78.

How to handle the show down. It's not easy teaching a student you're afraid of. Many students, especially males, have not gone through a rite of passage program. They think instilling fear in a female teacher is part of their rite of passage. There are many ways the showdown can play out in the classroom:

– Showdown 1: Teacher says unassertively, "Sit down." The student just won that showdown.

– Showdown 2: Teacher is inconsistent. The student wins all showdowns that they did not make a response.

– Showdown 3: Teacher becomes emotional, even hysterical, and begins to chase the student around the classroom. The student just won the showdown.

– Showdown 4: Teacher says, "I'm going to suspend you or send you to the only male staff person in the school." The student just won the showdown. Although he may lose to the male, he wins because he didn't give in and do what the teacher told him to do. He also got put out of class, which is ultimately what he wanted.

– Showdown 5: Teacher says in an assertive, no-nonsense tone of voice, "Sit down now." Teacher wins! It's not the race, gender, or size of the teacher that makes the difference but the tone of their voice and the fearless eye contact they make with the student. Effective teachers have excellent tone and give their students tough love and good eye contact.

– Showdown 6: Teacher is consistent, and they win. They respond to the student the same way each and every time. Children are confused when adults are inconsistent. If a child has a rope, he'll want to know how far along the rope he can go. When teachers respond differently each day of the week, children are confused. Each day they feel compelled to see how far they can take you on your rope. Effective teachers have a short, tight rope.

79.

Unity-Criticism-Unity (U-C-U).

(A) All the children form a Unity Circle. Rationale: Environment plays an important part in effecting behavior. Since we come together to help one another because we care for one another, a Unity Circle is most desirable.

(B) The coordinator or teacher of the session opens by saying, "Are there any words of praise?" Rationale: We come together to teach children how to find beauty in each other, complement and reward good behavior. This is especially satisfying to a child who was criticized during the last session but who has modified his or her behavior to the benefit of the collective.

(C) The teacher then asks, "Are there any criticisms?" In response to the teacher's question, the children raise their hands. This is done in an orderly manner. Any child who has an emotional outburst loses the chance for making a criticism. The teacher then records all hands raised. The role of the teacher is to coordinate, i.e. to make sure rules are followed, but not to take the disciplining of the child away from the collective. Rationale: We want to develop our children into logically thinking adults. We therefore expect a conversation which will not be filled with shouting and words of anger. We also wish to avoid criticism being given in reaction to a criticism placed upon someone. Our structure prevents the negative reaction of, "Since you criticized me I'm going to criticize you" from occurring. Criticisms are required to be given in a constructive way. We do not want children destroying each other. Only those children who have raised their hands are eligible to give criticism. Please also note that the children, so far, have only expressed that they have criticisms to give, but have not yet given it.

(D) The teacher then goes around the room to those who had raised their hands, seeking the nature of their concern. Again, any child who has an emotional outburst loses the chance to criticize. Rationale: We are trying to teach the children to communicate, to clearly express themselves. We also want a session where we think before we speak. By asking only for criticism at this time, the child who is being criticized has to think about it to himself or herself until we later ask for responses. We find that the immediate reacting to a criticism is defensive. We try to avoid that reaction by having some time elapse so that the child has to deal with it first before responding. A child who is being criticized and who speaks immediately in anger is also criticized for that, and sanctions are established, such as having the child write on paper the reason why he or she cannot control their temper, or having a letter sent home to the parent requesting a visit.

(E) The teacher will then ask the child who received the criticism, "What are your feelings about it?" The child answers by saying, "My feelings are . . ." A dialogue may develop

between the two children. This must be orderly.
No other children can speak without teacher
approval. Other children must also have
pertinent information to provide. A child
entering a discussion simply for the sake of the
discussion can also be criticized. When the
dialogue has ended, if action is then needed,
the teacher will ask the class what they feel the
punishment should be. A majority is needed in
any sanctions. Teachers must make sure that
the sanction is fair. This is done in the form of
suggestions. Rationale: The restriction of who

can enter into the discussion forces clarification of the issues. Teachers should moderate with this as the basic goal. Political science is taught through the voting procedure. Children feel the sanction is fair and correct when it comes from their peers. We find peer group pressure is much stricter than the pressure from teacher to child. Teachers should be cognizant of group members operating "behind the scene."

(F) At the completion of the UCU session we stand up in our Unity Circle and, through the creative of the teacher, a form of unity through song, chant, etc. is expressed.

80.

An eye for an eye. Unfortunately, Black/ Hispanic children have been taught that if someone hits you, hit them back. We must teach our children the consequences of this behavior. An eye for an eye will leave you blind. A tooth for a tooth will leave you toothless. Discuss with students the example of two well known gangs: the Bloods and the Crips. Their motto is "A life for a life." We start off with 100 Bloods and 100 Crips. One Blood is killed, one Crip is killed. If this continues, we will end up with only one person surviving out of 200. Ask students, "Do you really want to play the game 'an eye for an eye, a tooth for a tooth, a life for a life'?"

81.

Native American hand wrestling. Many of our children feel the only way to resolve conflict is by fighting. You can break up a fight in the classroom, but the students will merely take it out on the playground at recess, lunchtime, or after school. They'll take their fight across the street. It's not that they want to fight, but they feel they must resolve their conflicts *in public*. They must be validated as the best fighter in public. I'm not condoning fighting, but since we do need to resolve conflict, let's resolve it on our terms and under our control. Have students who are in conflict, at the end of the day and in front of their peers, sit down to a Native American hand wrestling competition. Students put their elbows on the desk, they grasp hands, and then attempt to put their opponent's arm down on the desk first. This will determine who's the strongest. Students can compete to see who can do the most pushups or run the fastest. How about a spelling bee or math contest? Too often I see children fighting and the adults turning a blind eye. That's not teaching them how to resolve conflict. Take control of the situation by putting students in a contest where no one will get hurt, and where both winner and loser can learn good sportsmanship.

82.

Snitching. If we want students to tell us what happened, then we need to protect them or they are not going to tell us what took place. It is also unfair for teachers to expect students to snitch on each other when teachers will not tell their principal about negative experiences that are taking place among the staff. Adults cannot have it both ways. If we want students to snitch on each other, then the staff needs to also snitch on each other.

CHAPTER 9: MALES

83.

Have male students sit in front. If you are unable to have your students sit in a circle with you in the center, then have the boys sit in the front of the class. Research shows that girls hear better than boys.

84.

Have boys stand at their desks. Many boys could complete their tasks if they didn't have to sit down for six hours during the school day. We need to pick and choose our battles. Let boys stand behind their desks and do their work. You might also want to place a favorite object, like a ball, in their non-writing hand while they're writing with the other. Research show this is calming and relaxes them.

85.

Exercise on the hour. Special education placements could be reduced if schools simply found creative ways to channel students' energy. Unfortunately, in many schools, physical education has been eliminated or only offered a couple of times a week because of budget cuts. One of the best ways to channel students' energy and reduce the number of boys being labeled ADD or ADHD is if, every hour on the hour, you have them exercise for five minutes. This is excellent for all students, especially boys. Movement can also reduce obesity among students.

86.

Let students sit on the floor. Students can learn sitting on the floor just as they can learn sitting at a desk for six hours. If your major objective is for students to do their work and if your boys like to read or do their work on the floor, why not let them do that. When you're at home reading, do you sit at a desk and read? Or do you like to get real comfortable on the floor, sofa, or bed? We need to create that kind of pleasurable learning environment for our students.

87.

Shorten your lesson plans. Research shows that boys have a shorter attention span than girls. When are teachers going to make the connection and shorten the lessons? You don't give a 60 minute lesson to students who have a 22 minute attention span. How long can your students focus on a lesson? That should determine how long the lesson will be.

88.

Schedule time for organizing. Many boys were telling the truth when they said they did their homework or they completed a particular assignment. They really did. The problem is, they couldn't remember where they put it. At least five minutes per day should be scheduled for organizing desks and notebooks and writing down homework assignments. Boys especially need to make organizing their materials a daily habit. This is a tremendous life skill that will help improve their academic performance as well as other areas of their lives.

89.

Provide male-oriented literature. Eighty-three percent of the boys in special education are not there because of ADD or ADHD. They're there because they're behind in reading. Ninety percent of inmates enter jail illiterate. Some governors determine prison growth based on fourth grade reading scores. It is obvious that reading ability is a precursor to many life experiences, positive and negative. Do we really understand how significant reading is for our male students? The million dollar question is, have we provided male students with literature that encourages them to read? Many boys have a disdain for reading because assigned books are not geared toward their interests. I encourage you to contact our company, African American Images. We have a set of books called "Best Books for Boys." Just specify the grade you want. If we know boys are interested in sports, hip hop, cars, and electronics, then classroom libraries should cater to their interests. Every female teacher should peruse the books they have and honestly assess whether the books would be stimulating to males.

90.

Cater to the male ego. To not understand the male ego is to not know your male students. The male ego is large and very insecure. Teachers should be careful about making derogatory comments about male students in front of their peer group. It is suicidal for a teacher to embarrass a male in front of his peers. Many teachers approach disciplining males like the military. They attempt to break them down then build them back up. Be careful about asking a male to read a story aloud if you're not sure he can handle that particular passage. Be careful about sending a male to the chalkboard to do work in front of the class if you're not confident he can handle the assignment.

91.

Understand the mama's boy. Unfortunately, some mothers raise their daughters and love their sons. You've probably noticed that your female students are more disciplined, responsible, and academically advanced than males. One reason for this is the double standard some mothers have in raising their sons and daughters. As a result, many boys think the adults in their lives—the principal, coach, judge, police, and teacher—are too hard on them. They believe their mothers are the only ones who truly care about them and will protect them. The boy wants you to lower your standards. You must convince this boy that your tough love is crucial to his growth and development.

92.

106 & Park. Watch *106 & Park* on BET and learn about the top 10 videos of the week. If you want to improve your children's writing skills, why not bring in the videos featured on *106 & Park*. Have students watch the video and then write about what they just observed. Remember, you want to improve their writing skills. They would love to write about what they enjoy, and they enjoy the videos featured on *106 & Park*. Use this assignment as a motivational carrot. If the students do well throughout the day, the last five or ten minutes will be allocated to *106 & Park*. There's also a good chance they'll perform much better during the school day if they know you're going to reward them with *106 & Park*.

93.

Put concepts to rap. Putting formulas, tables, ideas, thoughts, and theories to a jingle or song increases retention. Allow students to put your lessons to rap. Not only will this empower your students, but it's an excellent way to improve retention.

94.

Sagging.

- Did you know sagging started in prisons because men could not wear belts?

- Did you know in prison if your underwear shows it informs the inmates that you were a victim of a "booty" raid and are now available to any man for protection?

- How can a 50-year-old overweight police officer catch a 17-year-old male youth without a car, bike, gun, dog or

backup?

- Is it fair that some cities and institutions

  want to ban sagging?

- What are your chances of getting a job or

  a business loan sagging?

- Did you know saggin is the "N" word

  spelled backwards?

CHAPTER 11: PEDAGOGY

95.

Teach on your feet, not in your seat. We have too many tired teachers labeling children hyperactive. We need teachers who are healthy and have good attendance. Children need energetic, healthy teachers. Do everything you can to have perfect attendance.

96.

Rule 555.

95% of your problems come from 5% of your students. They occur either the first 5 minutes of the class or the last or 5 minutes of the class. Therefore empower the 5% to be your helper. Be ready to teach before students arrive. Assign additional work for fast learners during the last minutes of class.

97.

Give right brain tests. Earlier we mentioned installing learning centers in your classroom and the five ways to learn. For your more challenging students, periodically offer them a right brain test. You may be pleasantly surprised. The student who did not do well on a left brain, true-false, multiple choice exam may do very well on an oral exam. Let them take an object apart and put it back together and explain to you the function of each part.

98.

Let students ask most of the questions. Unfortunately, in many classrooms and schools, there's an inverse relationship between age and questions. As age increases, the number of questions decreases. It should be the opposite. As age increases, the questions asked should also increase. Create an environment in your classroom where students are encouraged to ask questions.

99.

Let students set the stage. Before some

students are able to settle down and get to work,

they have to set the stage. The desk must be

turned a certain way. Papers, pencils, and pens

need to be in a certain location. They have to

look around and see what their friends are

doing. This is a problem for teachers who run

their classes like a military operation. If the

student is not on task within the first 30 seconds,

they're then removed from the classroom. If

you allow students to set the stage, they become

your best students. If we simply allowed them a grace period of two or three minutes to set their stage, we may be very surprised at how well they perform.

100.

Create equal response opportunities for all students. Teachers call on some students more than others. To remedy this imbalance, get a package of index cards and two shoe boxes. Write the name of each student on an index card. When you want to call on a student, pull the name out of Box A; when the question is answered put the card in Box B. If you do this, there will be perfect distribution of response opportunities. Beware: students who were among the first to be called might figure out your system and realize they won't be called again until the rest of the class has been called. Reserve the right to pull their names out of Box B again if you see they are not staying on task.

101.

Offer feedback to all students. Research shows that students learn best when they're given feedback, reinforcement, and clues. Unfortunately, the research also shows that teachers give clues to some students more than others. Ironically, teachers say they have high expectations of all their students. Then why do we see the disparity in the amount of feedback given to various students? Make sure you give the same amount of feedback to each student.

102.

The buddy-buddy system. Twenty-eight students against one teacher—these are bad odds. One of the ways you can get more students on your side is to divide your students into competitive teams of two. The pairs will compete with other pairs. With the buddy-buddy system, you can pair peer tutors with students needing help. The system also can reduce disciplinary problems because students are responsible for each other.

103.

Cooperative learning. This is an expanded version of the buddy-buddy system. Divide the class into groups of four or five students and assign group projects. The jigsaw method is perfect for cooperative learning groups. Let's say we're having a lesson on Dr. King. Simply divide Dr. King's life into four parts: childhood, college, career, and family. Each member of the group will be responsible for a particular puzzle piece of information. The group is dependent on one another to provide a complete picture of information about the subject. Cooperative learning groups can also compete in spelling bees, math contests, and Black and Hispanic history bowls.

104.

Chess. Earlier we mentioned installing a gifted and talented area in your classroom. Chess games should be included in this area. There's excellent research on the benefits of playing chess. It improves the attention span, develops critical thinking skills, and gives students confidence. Every classroom should have chess games.

105.

Homework. Not only are students bored with school, they don't see the relevance of homework, especially when it takes two to four hours a night. First and foremost, homework should be meaningful. Secondly, it shouldn't take any longer than 30 minutes per subject to complete. What is the significance of doing 100 problems that have the same operations? Also, rotate the subjects so that students are not given 30 minutes in each subject each night. I recommend only a maximum of two subjects per night for a total of one hour per night.

106.

Return homework and classroom work in less than three days. Earlier we mentioned the importance of dignity and respect. If you want children to value academic performance, you sabotage your efforts if it takes you weeks and months to return assignments. Consider using your cooperative groups, buddies, or captain to help expedite the papers being returned on time. In addition, make sure you collect all assignments. It is unconscionable to assign students work and then not collect it. Students who are looking for reasons to not turn in assignments will say, "Why bother? She's not going to collect it anyway!"

107.

Test-Taking Techniques

1) Relax and encourage yourself throughout the exam. Tell yourself that you will earn a great score.

2) Get a good night sleep before the test.

3) Stay relaxed; if you begin to get nervous take a few deep breaths slowly to relax yourself and then get back to work.

4) Read the directions slowly and carefully.

5) If you don't understand the directions on the test, if possible, ask the teacher to explain.

6) Skim through the test so that you have a good idea how to pace yourself.

7) Write down important formulas, facts, definitions, and/or keywords in the margin first so you won't worry about forgetting them.

8) A student scored 79 when told it was a test and scored 121 when told it was a game. Think of the test as a game.

9) Finish the exam. Answer all questions, even if you have to guess.

10) Never stop for a long time on a question. Place a dot next to the question, and return if time permits. Answer the easy questions first.

11) Read all answers before deciding. The first answer has the least probability and the last

answer has the greatest. If you choose the first answer without reading all of them, you will not realize that the last answer included the first.

12) Use the process of elimination. There are five answers, and probably three of them do not make sense. You have a 50 percent probability with the remaining two answers.

13) Before reading the answers, ask yourself what the question is asking. Determine your answer first and then look for it in the answer key. Do not let multiple answers confuse you.

14) When in doubt, go with your first intuition.

15) Avoid careless mistakes. Place your answer in the right box. If time permits, check your work. Use all the time available. You do not score higher because you finished first.

16) Qualifiers like *never, always,* and *every* mean that the statement must be true all of the time. Usually these types of qualifiers lead to a false answer.

17) If any part of the question is false, then the entire statement is false, but just because part of a statement is true doesn't necessarily make the entire statement true.

18) Every part of a true sentence must be true. If any one part of the sentence is false, the

whole sentence is false, despite many other true statements.

19) Pay close attention to negatives, qualifiers, absolutes, and long strings of statements.

20) Negatives can be confusing. If the question contains negatives, such as *no, not,* and *cannot* drop the negative and read what remains. Decide whether that sentence is true or false. If it is true, it's opposite, or negative, is usually false.

21) Qualifiers are words that restrict or open up general statements. Words like *some-times, often, frequently, ordinarily,* and *generally* open up the possibilities of making accurate statements. They make more modest

claims, are most likely to reflect reality, and usually indicate true answers.

22) Absolute words restrict possibilities. *No, never, none, always, every, entirely,* and *only* imply the statement mustbe true 100 percent of the time and usually indicate false answers.

23) Long sentences often include groups of words set off by punctuation. Pay attention to the truth of each of these phrases. If one is false, it usually indicates a false answer.

24) In "All of the above" and "None of the above" choices, if you are certain one of the statements is true, don't choose "None of the above." If one of the statements is false, don't choose "All of the above."

25) In a question with an "All of the above" choice, if you see at least two correct statements, then "All of the above" is probably the answer.

26) If there is an "All of the above" option and you know that at least two of the choices are correct, select the "All of the above" choice.

27) Usually the correct answer is the choice with the most information.

28) Look for key words in test directions and questions such as: *choose, describe, explain, compare, identify, similar, except, not,* and *but.*

29) How can you avoid skipping a line on the answer sheet? Use a sheet of paper and line up your answers.

30) Many questions use the following words: *trace, support, analyze, explain, infer, summarize, evaluate, compare, formulate, contrast, describe,* and *predict.* You must know the meanings of these words.

CHAPTER 12: EPILOGUE

It's a Heart Condition

It's a Heart Condition——This class of 34 eighth graders had 5 teachers in the first 3 months of the school year. The teachers were African American, White, male and female, but each could not last with this class. They either quit or asked to be transferred. One teacher had been verbally abused and another had been punched. This was a very challenging class, and that's putting it mildly. They were 2 years behind academically and only 3 parents came to pick up their child's report card. They were all low-income and not one parent possessed a college degree.

Only 3 students had fathers in the home. The children lacked home training and basic common courtesy. And to make matters worse, a class size of 34 students is just too large. A teacher asked the principal if he/she could take over the class. Their race and gender are not important. This teacher knew what the students needed. The teacher told the students one thing that was very simple, but extremely important. He/she said, "I care about you." He/she then asked them to write their career goals and told them he/she would stay after school to help them to achieve their goals.

The teacher promised to visit each home. He/she managed to convince the students that they were family, by giving them hugs and strong words of encouragement. The class became the best disciplined and academically sound class in the school. When asked by the principal "how do you explain your success"? The teacher simply said, "it was never about the race or demographics of the students –it's a Heart Condition. You have to convince them that you care about them and then they will do whatever you ask of them."

I hope the strategies and activities presented in this book have been helpful, especially to Custodians, Referral Agents, Missionaries, and

Instructors. I know they have been helpful to Master Teachers and Coaches.

I would love to offer 100 more strategies and activities in a sequel to this book. If you have found strategies that have been effective and were not included in this book, please email me at <u>customer@africanamericanimages.com.</u> If your tip is selected for inclusion, you will receive full credit.

I wish you well during this school year, and I pray you will make a difference in the lives of children because they truly are a gift from God.

NOTES